Life in Tudor Times

✦

The Poor in Tudor England

Jane Shuter

Heinemann

First published in Great Britain by Heinemann Library
an imprint of Heinemann Publishers (Oxford) Ltd
Halley Court, Jordan Hill, Oxford OX2 8EJ

MADRID ATHENS PARIS
FLORENCE PRAGUE WARSAW
PORTSMOUTH NH CHICAGO SAO PAULO
SINGAPORE TOKYO MELBOURNE AUKLAND
IBADAN GABORONE JOHANNESBURG

© Jane Shuter 1995

Designed by Ron Kamen, Green Door Design Ltd, Basingstoke, Hampshire
Printed in Spain by Mateu Cromo Artes Graficas SA

99 98 97 96 95
10 9 8 7 6 5 4 3 2 1

ISBN 0 431 06750 3 [HB]

99 98 97 96 95
10 9 8 7 6 5 4 3 2 1

ISBN 0 431 06772 4 [PB]

British Library Cataloguing in Publication Data
Heinemann Our World Topic Books. - Life in Tudor Times. - The Poor in Tudor England
I. Shuter, Jane
942.05

Acknowledgements
The Publishers would like to thank the following for permission to reproduce photographs:
Bodleian Library: p. 15B
British Library: p. 9B
Christie's of London/Bridgeman Art Library: p. 21C, p. 27A
Edinburgh University Library: p. 23C
Fotomas Index: p. 13C, p. 29A
Hulton Deutsch Collection: p. 24A, p. 25B
Kunsthistoriches Museum, Vienna/Bridgeman Art Library: p. 11C
Museum of London: p. 12A
Peter Craven Photo Library, p. 19C
Victoria & Albert Museum: p. 17B

Cover photograph © Kunsthistoriches Museum, Vienna/Bridgeman Art Library

Our thanks to Mike Mullett of the University of Lancaster for his comments in the preparation of
this book.

Every effort has been made to contact copyright holders of any material reproduced in this book.
Any omissions will be rectified in subsequent printings if notice is given to the Publisher.

Money
12 pence (d) in a shilling (s)
20 shillings (s) in a pound (£)

CONTENTS

1 Who were the poor?

The poor in Tudor times were the people with the least money and power. There were many different types of poor people. Some were servants, **labourers** or **craftworkers** who did not have permanent jobs, but took on jobs by the day or the week. Some poor people worked and made just enough to live on. Others worked but made too little money to live on. Some poor people could not work, because they were disabled or could not find any work. Many poor people had times when they could manage. At other times they had to ask people for money. Some poor people even had times when they had to move to try to find work.

Types of poor people

Tudor people believed there were three types of poor. Firstly, there were people who had just enough to live on. Secondly came the **deserving poor**, people who could not work. This included people who were very young, very old, crippled or blind. People thought the deserving poor should be looked after, as it was not their fault that they could not work. The last group, called **sturdy rogues**, were people who were well enough to work, but who were not working. They were often **vagrants** – people who moved around looking for work. People said they should be punished for being lazy. They did not realize that there was not enough work.

There were more and more poor people in Tudor England as time went on. In 1485 there were almost as many jobs as workers. But by the 1530s there were more people looking for jobs than there was work to do. Some people understood this. But most people still thought that those who were out of work were lazy. The **monarchs** and their governments were scared that the poor, angry at their poverty, would rebel. There were some rebellions in Tudor times, but none of them succeeded. But the governments were worried enough to start to think about how to help the poor.

Source A

A king should take more care for the wealth of his people than for his own wealth. For where shall a man find more quarrelling than among beggars? Who wants changes more than those who are not content with their present life? Who is more likely to bring all into a hurley burley than they that have nothing to lose?

Written in 1551 by Sir Thomas More. More was an adviser to Henry VIII. He sympathized with many poor people, especially those who had been thrown out of their homes. But as well as feeling sorry for them he saw that they could be dangerous, because they had nothing to lose by rebelling against the government.

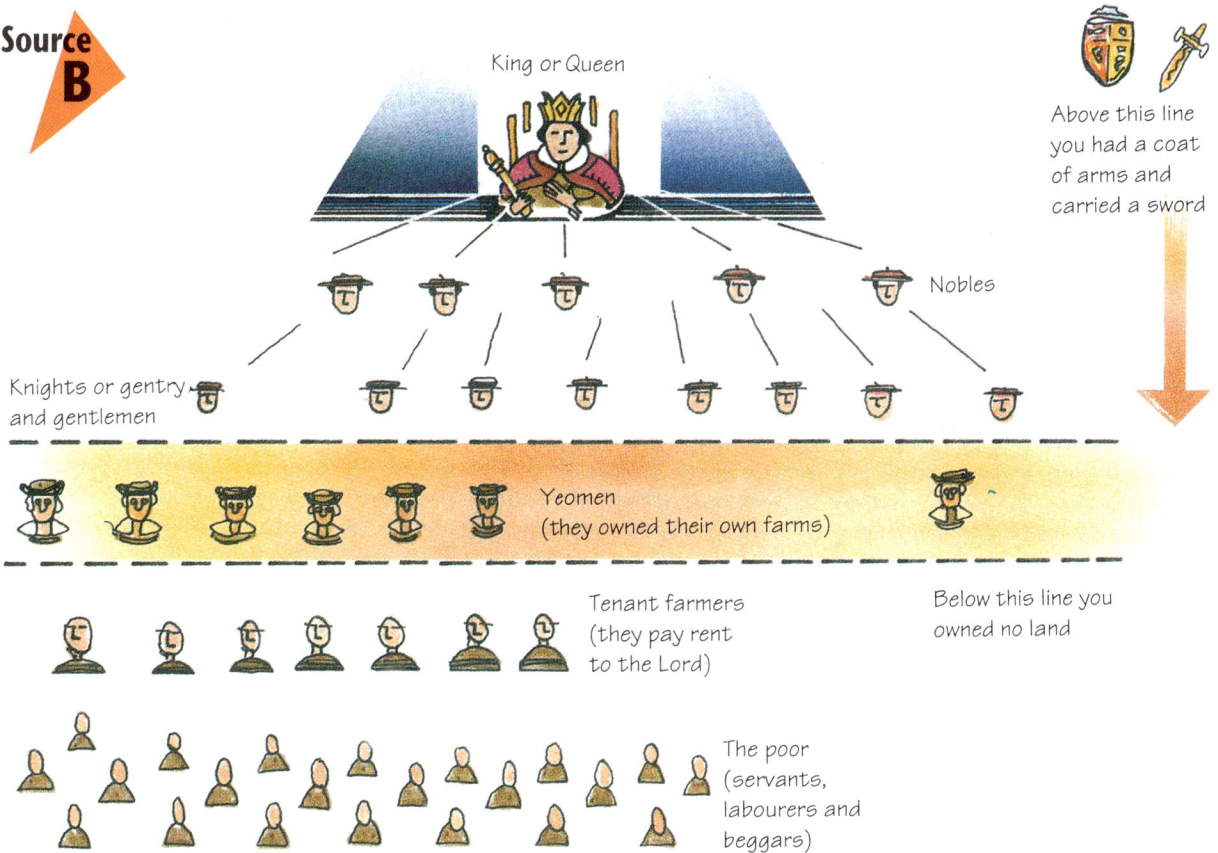

King or Queen

Above this line you had a coat of arms and carried a sword

Nobles

Knights or gentry and gentlemen

Yeomen (they owned their own farms)

Tenant farmers (they pay rent to the Lord)

Below this line you owned no land

The poor (servants, labourers and beggars)

This diagram shows how money and power were divided up in Tudor England. The monarch, at the top, has the most money and power. The poor, at the bottom, have hardly any of either.

Source C

The shortage of all things makes many people poor. Prices and **rents** are going up excessively. The number of poor people is also multiplying because the children of the poor often become poor themselves. A new sort of poor has also crept among us. There were always poor **lepers**, aged poor, sick poor, poor widows, poor orphans and suchlike, but now there are poor **soldiers** too.

Written by William Lambarde, a Justice of the Peace, in 1594. Lambarde, and the government, were worried by the large number of poor people who were also young, strong and even trained to fight.

Some incomes in 1570

The average income of **nobles** was between £2,000 and £3,000 a year.

The average income of a **gentleman** was between £500 and £700 a year.

The income of a craftworker was about £15 a year.

The income of a female servant was between £1 and £4 a year.

People were poor if their income was under £1 a year.

2 The deserving poor

The poor in towns

Tudor people agreed that the **deserving poor** should be helped. They were the people who could not work. They were too young, too old or too sick. There were also people who worked but did not earn enough to live on. The amount of help given to the poor varied from place to place and from time to time. There were always more poor people in towns than in the countryside. Poor people from the country often moved to the towns to look for work. They added to the numbers of poor people who were already there. Some towns, like Norwich, organized help for the deserving poor from the 1540s. They made better-off people give **alms** regularly. Lists were made of the town poor, and the most deserving were given alms.

There were 40 **households** on the 1570 list. They were mostly families, although there were widows and women who never married. In the families the men worked a little or not at all. Almost all the women and female children worked at home. They carded, spun and knitted wool to make cloth. They made lace and took in sewing. Only ten households were given alms in 1570. More of them needed alms when bread prices went up. Then there were more people needing alms than could be helped.

The Peel family and the Fulborne family were both on the poor list for Norwich for 1570.

The Peel family

Thomas Peel was 50 years old in 1570, as was his wife, Margaret. They were described as 'very poor' in the 1570 Norwich records. They had once lived in Yorkshire and been better-off. Thomas was **apprenticed** (sent to live with a **craftworker** to learn a **trade**) to a shoemaker when he was a boy. He then worked for himself making shoes. They had two children, born in 1554 and 1558. In 1562, for reasons that were not recorded, they left Yorkshire to look for work. They got as far as Norwich. Thomas found work and they **rented** a room in a house in St Stephen's parish. They had a third child in 1565. But Thomas did not make enough money to keep the family, so Margaret and their eldest child, a girl, helped by spinning wool at home for the clothmakers of Norwich. The other two children, probably both boys, went to school rather than working. The Peels were not given alms.

The Fulborne family

Alexander Fulborne and his wife Agnes, both 40 years old in 1570, had lived in Norwich all their lives. Alexander had been apprenticed to a tailor as a boy. He was out of work in 1570. Agnes knitted to make money. Their daughters, aged seventeen and twelve, spun wool. They were given alms of 2d a week. Like the Peel family, they were described as 'very poor' in the records. They were given money, while the Peels were not. Maybe this was because the Peels sent their boys to school and the **officials** thought they should be working too.

A Tudor print of poor people begging for money. They are all deserving poor, unable to work. The man on the left is crippled. The man on the right is blind. The woman is a widow with three children to feed and care for. She would find it hard to work too. Tudor people felt it was right to help these people.

There were poor families struggling in the countryside too. Until 1572, help in the countryside was run by the **parish**, using money given by people as a gift or in **wills**. There was not often enough money to help all who needed it. Parish officials visited the parish poor and decided who needed help the most. Parishes had to look after old people and the disabled. A lot of their money was spent on caring for children who had no family to look after them.

There were also people in the parish who said they could not keep everyone in the family. The parish paid someone else to look after these children until their parents could afford to have them back.

William Fox

William Fox was thirteen in 1598. He is listed in the parish records for Shorne in Kent as 'lame in both legs', and was said to have to 'go about on stilts'. He had no family. The parish officials paid a local family to look after him. The next year they bought him a new shirt but decided they did not want to support him any longer. There were laws against begging, but they did allow disabled people to beg. The parish wrote a **licence** for William, allowing him to beg locally. He went begging, but did not make enough to manage very well. In 1602 the parish paid £6 to a **hospital** to take him in and look after him. They also spent 9s on clothes for him so that he would arrive looking well cared for.

3 Sturdy rogues

A **sturdy rogue** was someone who was fit and well, able to work, but not working. Sturdy rogues were usually **vagrants** – people who moved round the country looking for work. Other people were seen as vagrants too. Travelling entertainers and tinkers were called vagrants, even though some of them were earning a living. Vagrants were seen as lazy, dishonest and dangerous. Most Tudor people saw vagrants as far more dangerous than they were. Historians know that they included ordinary families and people who were only out of work for part of the year.

How people saw vagrants

Vagrants travelled mostly in small groups. But people who wrote about them at the time saw them as large gangs of people. They thought vagrants had their own language and habits and were set against honest people. Some people feared that vagrants might start a riot, or even a rebellion against the government. It did not help that many of them were strong young men – they looked dangerous. It also did not help that some of them were soldiers or sailors travelling home after they had left the army or navy, and some of them carried weapons. It also did not help that some of them were really not looking for work. They were really begging when they did not need to, or stealing for a living.

Source A

I thought it my duty to tell you of the wicked and detestable behaviour of all of these ragged rabble who – under the pretence of great misery, **disease** or disaster – manage to gain **alms** from good people in all places.

Written by Thomas Harman (a Justice of the Peace) in 1567. Harman wrote a book describing various sorts of cheating vagrants. Books about people who tricked money out of other people were popular at the time. Harman's book was based on one of these, written to make money. He believed the story, but it may have been made up, and so his book could be wrong.

Some real vagrants

Thomas Luffkin was arrested in 1558 in Maidstone. He was travelling from place to place claiming that he could cure all sorts of diseases. He was accused of faking and punished.

John Wilson and his wife Agnes were among 23 vagrants arrested on one night in August 1571 in a village in Nottinghamshire. They had a **licence** to travel selling various things and so were released. Another couple were released, for the same reason. Everyone else was punished.

Margaret Holden was a dressmaker from Warwick. She was arrested as a vagrant in Shrewsbury in 1600. She explained that she travelled from market to market to find work, but was still punished.

Nicholas Jennings – fact or fiction?

This story comes from Thomas Harman's book about vagrants, *A Caveat for Common Cursitors*, printed in 1567 (see Source A and the caption). Many people have believed Harman, because he was a JP and asked real vagrants about their lives. But we must be careful of his evidence. He believed what he said, but based his questions on a book which was made up. He often offered vagrants a meal if they answered his questions. They might have agreed to anything to be fed. Certainly historians have found that most vagrants were very poor and looking for work. They were not all professional cheats, as Harman suggested.

Harman said he met a beggar in London who was dressed in rags and covered in blood and dirt, pretending to be ill. The beggar said his name was Jennings. Jennings told Harman he had fits and had been in Bedlam, a **hospital** for mad people. Harman sent a note to Bedlam, to ask if Jennings had even been there. They said no. So Harman told his printer, and the printer sent two **apprentices** to follow Jennings. He spent all day begging in London, secretly putting more blood and dirt on himself as it wore off. When he went home one boy followed him, the other fetched the printer.

Jennings in his two disguises, a picture from Harman's book.

The printer fetched a **constable** and they caught and searched Jennings. He had made 13s 4d, exactly 20 times as much as a carpenter would have for a day's work. They made him wash and found he was not at all ill or disfigured under the blood and dirt. They shut him up for the night in a tavern, but he escaped. A few weeks later the printer saw a man he was sure was Jennings, much better dressed but still begging. The printer asked who he was. Jennings gave the same name, but this time said he was a hat-maker who just needed money to pay for a room for the night. He would find work with the London hat-makers next day. The printer had him arrested. He was whipped and put in the **pillory** for the day and then into prison. He was let out after promising to live honestly.

4 Childhood and education

The children of the poor where very likely to die of some **infectious disease** before they were one year old. Poor babies grew up in homes that were cold, damp and draughty.

Poor people could often not afford to feed all their children. Sometimes they left their babies in churches so that the **parish** would bring them up. Parishes got into regular arguments over who was to care for orphans. Other poor people kept their children but asked the parish to care for some of them, until the father found work or the family managed to earn more money somehow. The town or parish **officials** would arrange for them to live with someone else.

Parish apprentices

The officials were keen to find the boys work as **apprentices**. They agreed to work free for a **master** for seven years to learn his **trade**. Then they could set up in business on their own, if they could afford it. Most poor boys could not. They worked for a master for a weekly wage instead. The parish officials hoped that if poor boys learned a trade they could support themselves.

Poor people had just as many children as the better-off. But the average number of children in a poor family was often as low as three. The rest were dead, abandoned, being cared for by the parish or working somewhere else.

Source A

Children should be taught to pray and say the Ten Commandments in their own language. They should be taught whatever will to fit them for an occupation, rather than left in idleness.

From a message sent to the clergy in 1536. It was sent in the name of the King, Henry VIII, but was written by one of his ministers, Thomas Cromwell. It does not say all children should go to school, but it does say they should be taught a skill.

Source B

We put out the following children of the poor of this parish to be apprentices:
Solomon Farne, aged 12
[The word 'died' is added later, in a different handwriting.]
Agnes Farne, aged 9 years
John Saunders, aged 9
[The word 'died' is added later, in a different handwriting.]
George Adams, aged 14
Prudence Horseley, aged 9
John Lark, aged 12
One of Stockwell's children, we know not his exact age nor does Stockwell or his wife.

From the Parish Records of Shorne, Kent, for 1598. Usually only boys became apprentices. Agnes Farne and Prudence Horseley were probably trained as female servants. We do not know what the boys died of, but we can see the parish kept a check on them, even once they were apprentices.

Education

What the children who stayed at home did depended on whether they were boys or girls. Like most other people at the time, poor parents sent boys to school if they could. They expected girls to stay at home and learn how to run a house. This often meant that girls and their mothers worked at home to earn some money. The boys went to the local school for the poor. Things were different in the countryside. Schools were often far away and harder to get to. Even if poor country boys did have a school nearby, they only went to it when they were not needed to help with the farm work.

The Distinguished Visitor, **painted by Jan Breugel in 1600. It shows a well-off man and his wife and servant visiting a poor family. The wife is about to give a child some money, the servant is carrying a basket, which could have food in it. Although this is a Dutch painting things were very like this in Britain too.**

5 Working in towns

Poor people often only worked some of the time. They had to take work that did not need any special skills and which paid very badly. This was the case even if they had been better-off and had been trained to do a skilled job.

Working at a trade

Records of the poor in Tudor towns tell us most about families. Poor men who had trained to a **trade** often spent a lot of time trying to find work in that trade. The women of the family took in all sorts of jobs at home to make money. The men often had to take low paid jobs in their trade. A 1570 survey of the poor in Norwich showed John Hubbard, a butcher, worked in a **slaughterhouse**. Roger Stevenson had trained as a cap-maker, but worked in the same trade making cap patterns.

Any job will do?

Poor men in the towns also worked as **watchmen** and cleaned the rubbish and **sewage** from the streets. Some of them stood on the streets at night, hoping someone would pay them to light their way home through the dark streets. Very few poor people had regular work. They often had to mix work and begging if the **parish officials** would not give them **alms**. Whole families were always trying to find ways to make a few pence. They tried to get work in the nearby countryside at harvest time.

Source A

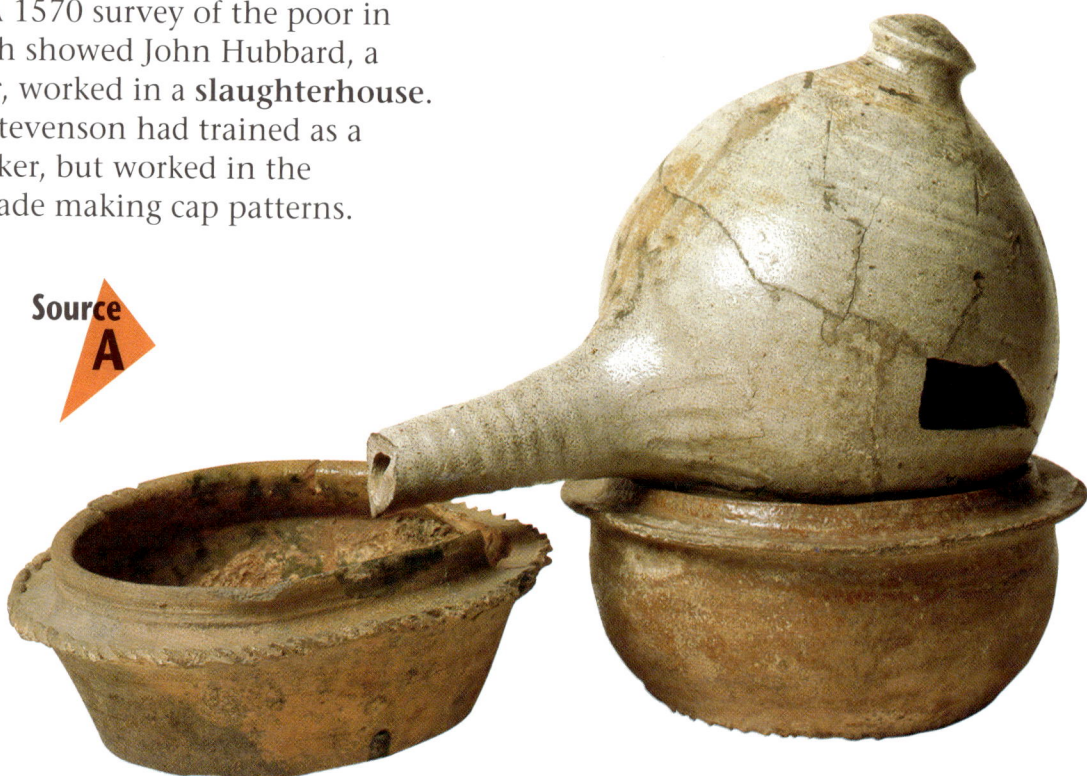

Poor people tried to make money at home. They would use equipment like this to make drink to sell to people who came to the house to get it. This was against the law, but many people took the risk.

Mark Lewis of London, a pinner by trade, says on 14 August 1595 he left London to look for harvest work. He met John Stafford, a man he knew as a soldier in France. When they reached Sutton, Stafford told him to wait outside the town. Stafford went into the town and came back with a bundle of stuff which he said they would sell and divide what they made. He said they should split up and meet later, since when he has not seen Stafford.

Evidence collected from a man accused of robbery, before he went to Maidstone for trial. Poverty often forced people to steal. Lewis says he did not take part in the robbery but would have shared the loot. His trial records did not survive, so we do not know what happened to him.

Driven to crime?

Stealing was the crime in 43 out of 64 cases dealt with by the local courts in Hertfordshire in 1596. This was after two years of bad harvests. Food prices had gone up sharply. The people accused were mostly poor people, **labourers** or town workers.

In 1591 there had been 52 cases. Only 22 were of stealing. Of these, the people accused were, again, mostly poor people.

Source C

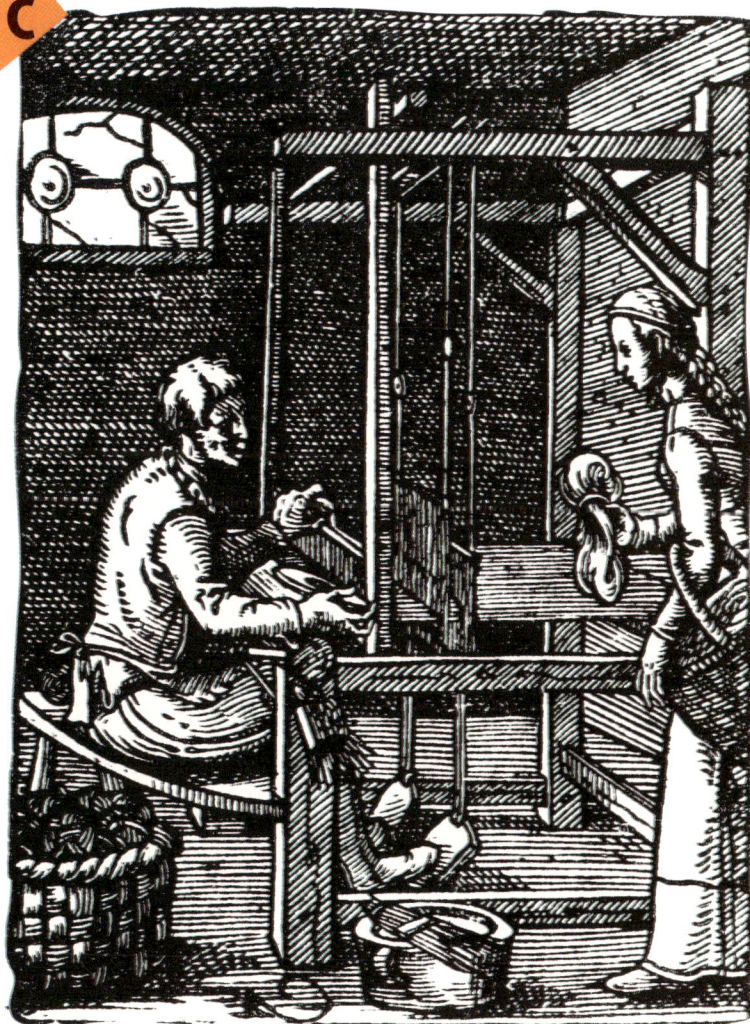

A sixteenth-century print showing a weaver and his wife working at home. They were lucky to have the loom to work on. The person they were working for either gave them the spun wool to weave, or gave them the wool and the wife spun while the husband did the weaving.

6 Working in the country

The country poor worked in the fields, doing different jobs at different times of the year. The lucky ones had permanent jobs and homes that went with the job. These homes often had gardens. People could grow their own food and keep a few chickens. But many poor people were **labourers** who had no permanent job. They either hired themselves out in the same place from day to day or travelled looking for work. Often, they only worked at times when farmers needed more workers than usual, like harvest time. So, for part of the year at least, they had no work and nowhere to live. This meant they would be treated as **vagrants**.

Why move on?

Country people who lost their jobs often moved to the town to look for work. In one way this was sensible, especially if they could find a place to stay. Then the town **officials** might give them **alms**. Even a slight chance of work would draw them to the towns. But the towns were already crowded with their own poor, many of them with useful skills. So it was unlikely that a labourer would find a job. Still, many of the poor who moved around looking for work kept moving on, hoping that in the next town, or at the next farm, someone would give them work.

Source A

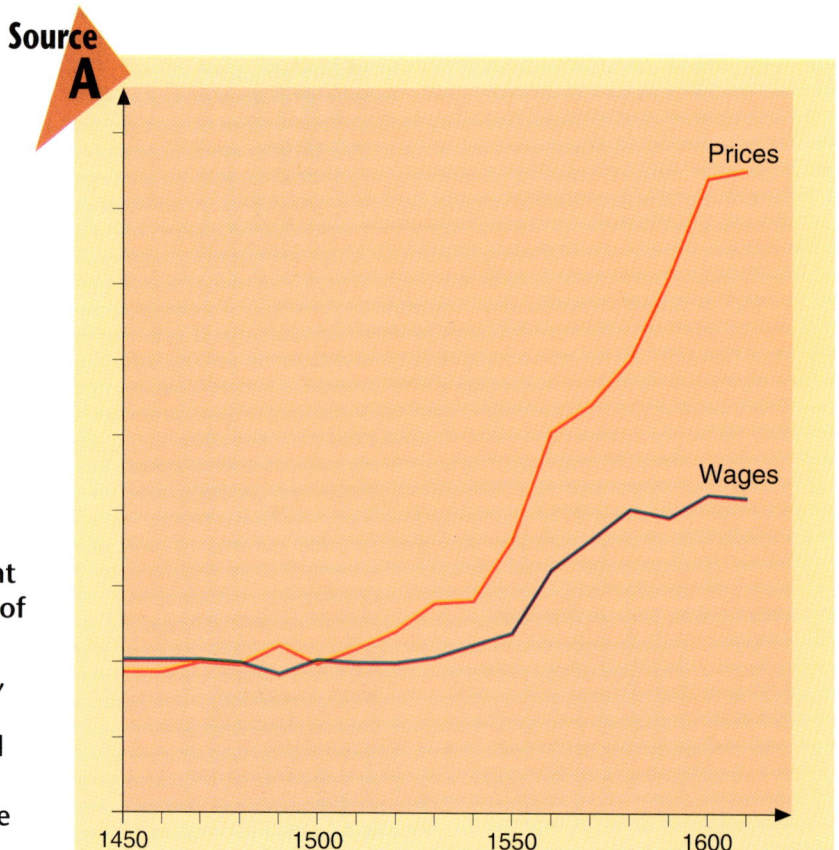

As the graph on the right shows, while the wages of a poor farmworker rose between 1485 and 1603, prices rose much faster. Even if a farmworker did not lose his job, it got harder and harder to live on his wages.

Changing fortunes

People often worked some of the time and were out of work at other times. Sometimes they were much better-off than others. Humphrey Gibbons was arrested as a vagrant in New Romney in 1596. He said in 1586 he was married with a large farm. But, in 1591, he had been forced by rising prices and bad harvests to sell his farm. He moved around east Kent labouring by the day. He did this for three years, and saved enough to **rent** a small farm in 1594. In 1596 the harvest failed. He had to go back to labouring, and was looking for work.

This picture is from the front page of a book on growing herbs, printed in 1597. Country labourers who went to the towns to look for work did not often get any. If they were lucky they might find work for a while working on a rich man's garden, like the gardeners shown here.

7 Marriage and family life

How old poor people were when they married depended on how much they wanted to live on their own. Some couples waited until the man had a job and a house. Indeed, some women refused to marry until then. They said that they did not want to live with their husband's family. This meant that they left marrying until very late, often until their mid-twenties.

Poor couples often chose who they married for themselves. But the average time that a poor couple lived together was just seven years. This was partly because they left marrying so late. But it was mostly because the chance of one of them dying within seven years of marriage was very high. Families were not together for long either. Children had often left home to work by the age of ten.

Couples and families did not often go looking for work together. There were several reasons for this. Life on the road was hard. Often the husband looked for work and sent for his family when he found some. But sometimes husbands went off and never came back. In the 1590s, Katherine Knight of Hythe was arrested as a **vagrant**. She and her husband worked in different places, wherever they could find work.

These charts show the sorts of people who were arrested as vagrants. Most of them were single young people. Families were less likely to be arrested than sturdy rogues. This may make it look as if there were fewer families on the road than there were.

Problems of poverty

Poverty often drove men to despair, and sometimes to drink. This often caused trouble between a husband and his wife. In 1583, Jane Saffrey, wife of Nicholas Saffrey of Dover, said her husband beat her so hard that he drew blood 'for no other cause than her asking for money to provide bread for her and her children'. When she went to fetch him out of a beer house, where he had been drinking, he threatened to knock her over. In the same week he gave another beer house keeper his tools in return for drink.

Source A

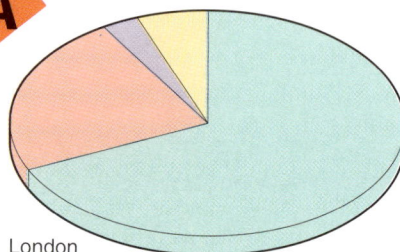

London

Norwich

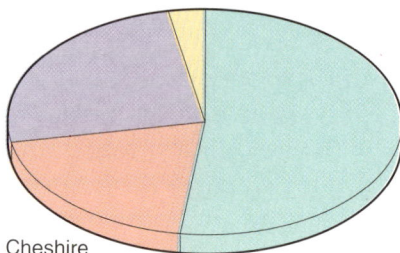

Cheshire

Single men
Single women
Married couples
Children under 7

Part of a sixteenth-century cushion cover that shows country life.
The poor man and his wife are working together to harvest fruit.
They are supposed to be poor people, but are much better
dressed than many poor people would have been, to make the
picture prettier.

8 Houses and homes

The houses of poor people were small, draughty and cramped. The floors were often just earth beaten flat and covered with straw. Very few of them have survived for us to know what they looked like. The houses for the poor in towns were often put up quickly and fell down (or burned down) just as quickly. They were mostly made of wood with thatched roofs.

How many rooms?

The poorest country people lived in one-roomed homes. They were put up quickly (a Cumberland man once said **labourers'** houses could be put up in just three or four hours) and few have survived. Historians have studied the **wills** and inventories (lists of possessions) of labourers. They have found almost all labourers lived in one-roomed houses. The others were most likely to live in two-roomed houses. However, this varied a lot around the country. People were more likely to have more rooms if they lived in the south or east of England.

Living rough

Some poor people who lost their jobs went to live in the woods rather than going to look for work. They made themselves houses from mud and branches. These houses were described as **hovels** by some people. They were probably not much worse than the homes the poor had left.

Source A

Cottages are built with walls of earth, low thatched roofs, no floor boards, few walls inside and no glass windows. There are very few with chimneys except a hole in the roof to let the smoke out.

From *A Description of Cornwall*, written by Richard Carew in 1602. Cottages were made of different things in different parts of the country, depending on how much wood was available and how much straw there was for thatching.

Source B

There are old men today who say that they, not poor men, would have slept on straw covered with a sheet, under a single rough cover. They would have had a good round log under their head as a pillow. They would have been glad of a sheet to cover themselves with, they would have had nothing to protect them from the pricking straw under them. A feather mattress would have been a wonder to them, and as for pillows they were for women in childbirth.

Written in 1577, by William Harrison in his book, *A Description of England*. Harrison was grumbling about how people in the 1570s expected to have more possessions than their fathers and grandfathers did. It is probably a fair description of how the poor lived in the 1570s.

Source C

Almshouses for the poor at Windsor Castle. Almshouses were built to house the **deserving poor** by better-off people or by the **parish**. People often left money in their wills to build and repair these houses, so that local poor would have somewhere to live. These are big almshouses. Many of them were smaller and only one storey high.

Possessions of the poor

It is not easy to say what poor people owned – the easiest answer is 'very little'. The wills of labourers and poor townspeople only show what the better-off poor owned. The really poor made no wills. But wills make some things clear. The most important things the poor owned were tools. They needed tools to be able to work at all. A poor carpenter in Rye in 1592 left only his tools, a cauldron (cooking pot) two spoons, a knife and a piece of bacon in the chimney. A farm labourer in Ash in 1593 left fifteen farm tools (scythes, rakes and spades). Other than this he left a blanket, a cauldron, two pans and other things worth 6d. Poor people did not have much furniture. They might have a table and stools to sit on, if they were lucky. They slept on a mattress made out of bundles of straw which they laid on the floor. The most common possession after tools was a cooking pot.

9 Food and drink

Poor people had very little choice of food. What they ate depended partly on where they lived and how poor they were. There were some things that were always the same.

Poor people ate very little meat. They probably never drank wine. Most of their food was cooked in one big pot. It was a mixture of whatever they could grow, buy or beg. Sometimes it was just a thin porridge made out of oats. At other times they might catch birds (like pigeons) or animals (like rabbits) in the woods. Then they had meat to go in the pot. Most of the time they drank a watered-down version of beer, called small beer.

Vagrants and beggars

Vagrants often carried a cooking pot with them. They made a fire when they stopped walking for the day. This would not always be possible. Sometimes there was too much rain to get a fire to light. In this case they had to eat what they had raw, even if it was something like turnips.

Beggars lived on leftover food from the kitchens of various houses. Poor people could often get bargains in the town market at the end of market day. People often sold things cheaply rather than carry them home, especially things that might go bad, like butter and fish.

Source A

A poor countryman is pleased if he has enough land to grow cabbages, radishes, parsnips, carrots, melons, pumpkins. This is all that he and his **household** can have to eat. They would eat bread made from wheat, if they could afford it. But they cannot, so they have it made from oat or barley flour.

Written by William Harrison, in his book, *A Description of England*, published in 1577.

Source B

The most important food of the poor was bread. Next to this came cheese, lard and milk. If they ate meat at all it would be bacon, bought from a better-off neighbour when they killed their pig, and hung in the chimney to be preserved by the smoke. The rest of his food came from his garden. The poor drank ale and beer. They also drank milk from cows, sheep or goats.

Written by the historian, Alan Everitt in *The Agrarian History of England and Wales*, published in 1967. Everitt looked at lists of what farmworkers owned when they died. These lists were very detailed, and often included the food in the house.

Source
C

The Harvesters' Meal, painted by the Dutch artist, Peter Breugel, in the sixteenth century. The people are eating bread and porridge. They are probably drinking small beer. The painting is of Dutch people, but the meal is like meals described by English poor.

10 Entertainment

Poor people had very little time for entertainment. They had to spend most of their time working or looking for work. Entertainment needed to be cheap or free, for they did not have much money to spare.

Popular entertainments with the poor that did not cost anything were **cock-fighting** and ratting. It might be expensive if they decided to bet on who won, though. Football was also popular, although it was not like a game of football now. Descriptions of football matches at the time sound as though there were no rules at all! All these sports needed only a piece of clear ground. They used things people had already. In London, people stood to watch a play in a theatre for 1d. A **labourer's** wage was about 3d a day and some poor people earned less than this.

Special occasions

Special occasions often gave the poor free entertainment. Market day in the nearest town offered lots of things to see and do. **Fairs** also provided free entertainment. Travelling players often followed fairs and put on shows. They sent people round with a hat to collect money from the people watching, but it was easy to slip away without paying. Christmas and May Day also gave poor people days when they could rest and enjoy themselves (Source A).

Source A

Everyone in every **parish**, town and village gathers together, men women and children, old and young. They go into the woods or the hills and collect branches to decorate their feast and a Maypole which they cover with flowers, herbs and strings. Sometimes it is even painted several colours. They raise it up, put straw on the ground around it and fall to feasting and dancing around the Maypole.

A description of May Day celebrations, held on 1 May, written by Philip Stubbes in 1583. Stubbes was a preacher who was against celebrations like this because he thought they stopped people worshipping God.

Source B

When the boggy land on the north side of the city is frozen many young men play on the ice. Some slide in wide strides, others make themselves seats of ice as big as millstones. Then one sits down and the others pull and push him. Some tie bones to their feet and shove themselves along with sticks. Sometimes two of them run at each other with poles, and hit each other and fall.

Written by John Stowe, in his book, *A Survey of London*, in 1598. Swimming, wrestling and racing were also free and were, like skating, popular sports with poor young people.

This picture shows some better-off people watching the fighting in a specially built pit with seats. Cock-fights could be held on any piece of open space, often with the audience acting as a barrier to keep the cocks in the centre. This was how poor people watched cock-fighting.

A dangerous game

A law was passed in 1541 which made it illegal for poor men to play football except at Christmas time, or on their **master's** property with his permission. Football was played mainly in fields, but could be played with goals at either end of a village (or even in different villages), which made it a mix of cross-country running and football. The ball could be kicked or carried, and goals could be scored by hitting any named target. There were no rules about not fighting. The fine for breaking the 1541 law was 40s a game. This was half a year's pay for a **labourer**. So **constables** ignored any games that broke out, unless someone died, when they had to be investigated by a special coroner's court. There were four cases of this in Essex between 1558 and 1603. In all four cases a man died in a game played in a field, as a result of players fighting or crashing into one another. The players involved in the fights were fined according to what they could pay.

11 Health

Poor people were very likely to become ill. Sometimes they did not have enough to eat. They might be given food by better-off people. This was often leftovers, going bad. If this was all they had then they ate it anyway. They lived in the worst parts of towns or villages, in damp, cold homes. Their houses were often crammed with people, so **infectious diseases** spread easily.

When poor people were ill they often did not get better. Their bodies were less able to fight diseases. They could not afford to buy any medicines or special food to help them get better. They could not send for a doctor when they were sick. Sometimes poor people in a town could ask the **apothecary** for advice. Apothecaries sold medicines, herbs and spices. They might give free advice. They charged for any medicines they thought sick people needed. Some places had people (usually women) living nearby who knew about using herbs and wild fruits and plants to cure sickness.

Poor people who were **vagrants** were less likely to get help when they were sick. If they got too sick to keep travelling they just lay down in a doorway or under a hedge. They stayed there until they either got better or died.

Source A

This sixteenth-century print shows a doctor visiting a patient. The doctor is the man standing next to the patient. The person moving the leg is the doctor's assistant. Doctors charged a lot of money to visit a patient. They also charged for any medicine they gave. Poor people could not afford a visit like this.

This sixteenth-century print shows women helping at the birth of a baby. The family in this picture are not poor, they have wooden floors and lots of carved furniture. But poor women also went to help when another woman was having a baby. A poor family could not pay for a doctor to help. It was treated almost like a social event.

Source C

About 15 January Richard Riplingham visited the JP Sir Nathaniel Bacon, to ask what was the best thing to do with a vagrant boy of about ten or twelve years. He was in Warham and was sick. Sir Nathaniel said the boy was over seven years old, so a vagrant. If he was well enough he must be given a **passport** to go back to where he was born. Riplingham said the boy was not very ill. He went back to Warham, put the boy in a cart and took him out of the town. The boy died in the cart and Riplingham left him by the roadside.

Part of the evidence given in court against Riplingham in 1593. He was prosecuted for not telling Sir Nathaniel the truth about how sick the boy was and for treating the boy inhumanely.

12 What did the government do? 1

Tudor **monarchs** and governments passed many Poor Laws to deal with the poor. The way that they treated the poor changed as they saw the problems the poor faced. The laws usually dealt with both the **deserving poor** and the **sturdy rogues**. Because they treated each group differently we will look at the things they did for each group separately.

The deserving poor were always treated more kindly. Early Poor Laws allowed the deserving poor to beg. At first the government expected better-off people to give money and food. This did not work. So the government made the **parish** care for the deserving poor. Better-off people were made to give money to help them.

What Tudor Poor Laws did for the deserving poor

1495 Local deserving poor can beg in their own parish but nowhere else.

1531 Local deserving poor can still beg in their own parish but must have a **licence** from their **JP** to beg.

1536 People must not give directly to any poor people without a licence, but to the parish church **officials** who will give to the most deserving.

1547 Local deserving poor can beg with a licence. The parish must find homeless deserving poor a place to live, building houses if necessary. A collection for the poor must be made after church on Sunday. No one *has* to give.

1552 No one can sit outdoors and beg. Licensed beggars can still go from door to door in their parish. Special officials take the Sunday collection and make lists of those who give money and who it is given to. People not forced by law to give money.

1563 If people do not give money to the Sunday collection they have to explain why not to their JP. If they do not have a good reason the JP can put them in prison. A check is kept on the collectors to make sure they are taking in and giving out poor money regularly. Priests must make sure that there is a collection and must remind people to give money, or they will be fined. Disabled poor people can still beg from door to door if they have a licence. Other poor people have to rely on **alms** from the parish.

1597 **Overseers** of the poor are appointed to run all care for the poor, including making sure they have somewhere to live. The parish officials set a poor **rate** and tell everyone what they must give to the overseers. If they do not pay, the overseers can take any possessions that are worth the amount of the rate, and sell them to get the money.

The Seven Acts of Mercy, painted in about 1600 by the Dutch painter Peter Breugel. The deserving poor are being given bread. Dutch people and British people did this. People sometimes left money in their **wills** to be spent to give bread to the poor on a particular day each year. Until 1536 beggars could rely on some charity from monks and nuns up and down the country. From 1536 on the monasteries were closed and this charity was lost.

No person or clergyman shall feed any beggars at their doors, in pain of the fine laid down by the law. More than this they shall pay an extra 4d each time, to be collected by church officials. This money will go to relieve the poor of this city.

Part of the orders for the poor made by Norwich council in 1571. Beggars and vagrants moved to large towns such as Norwich to find work, food and alms. Many people in the towns were also out of work. These towns made extra arrangements for looking after the poor.

13 What did the government do? 2

Tudor governments tried to deal with **sturdy rogues** in several ways. The 1495 Poor Law said earlier laws against vagrants were too harsh. Those who were caught only had to sit in the **stocks**. But the number of **vagrants** went up. The government began to worry that the vagrants would rebel.

So laws got harsher and harsher. At first, the Poor Laws just punished vagrants. But the 1576 Law, and the ones that followed it, saw that vagrants might be unable to find work. They provided them with work and a place to work in. If they refused to do this, or went back to the vagrant life, they were punished.

What Tudor Poor Laws did to sturdy rogues

1495 Vagrants to be punished in the stocks for three days.

1531 Vagrants to be whipped.

1536 Vagrants to be made to work on jobs like road repairs in the **parish**.

1547 Vagrants could be forced to work as slaves, for anything from two years to the rest of their lives.
[This law was cancelled for being too harsh in 1549. The 1536 law was brought back.]

1572 Vagrants over 14 were to be whipped and have a hole made in their right ear the first time they were caught. If caught after this they were treated as criminals. They could be put in prison, even hanged.

Vagrants aged 5–14 could be made to become **apprentices**.

1576 Work provided for vagrants by parish. Houses of Correction (Bridewells) set up for people who refuse to work, run with money from the poor **rates**. They were forced to work and live here.

1597 **Overseers** of the poor appointed to run all care for the poor, including the Houses of Correction.

1597 *[a second Poor Law]*
Vagrants to be whipped and sent back to the county they last lived in. They had to go to the House of Correction, or take work. Houses of Correction to be set up in all towns and counties. Laws to cover people wandering without work or who refuse to work at a legally set wage. Vagrants who keep getting caught were sent overseas to work in the **colonies**.

A Tudor print which shows a vagrant being whipped through the streets of a town. This was the penalty for being arrested as a vagrant for the first time. In the background on the left you can see a hanging. This was the penalty for being arrested as a vagrant more than three times.

So that young people may be brought up in the habits of work, and not become idle rogues, and so that those who are rogues at the present may not have any just excuse to say that they cannot get work, and so that any who is poor and needy can have work, we order the setting up of a store of wool or other stuff to work with in all our cities and towns, which can be given to those who say they have no work.

Part of the 1576 Poor Law, called 'An Act for the Setting of the Poor on Work'. It was the first Poor Law to admit that vagrants, or sturdy rogues, might be telling the truth when they said they could not find work.

GLOSSARY

alms money or food given to the poor

almshouse a house built for poor people to live in, usually without paying any rent

apothecary a shopkeeper who sells herbs, spices and medicine

apprentice a boy learning a craft, working for a master

cock-fighting making two cockerels fight each other

colony a group of people from one country living in another country which belongs to the country they come from

constable A person, chosen by the people of a town or village, who makes sure people keep the law. Constables in Tudor times were not part of a big police force. They were not paid much, and were often old men who could find no other work.

craftworker a person who has the skill of making something

deserving poor poor people who could not work because they were too young, too old, sick, crippled or not able to work as they have children to look after

disease sickness

fair Where people get together to trade things, like horses. Entertainers and people selling food go there too.

gentleman a man with an income of between £500 and £700 a year

hospital A place where travellers and the poor could go for a bed to sleep in and food to eat for free. Some hospitals also looked after the sick, but it was not their main job and not all hospitals did this.

household everyone who lives in a house, including the family and their servants, and the things in the house

hovel house that is dirty, badly built, cramped and uncomfortable

infectious easily spread from one person to another

inventory A list of all of a person's possessions. In Tudor times inventories were usually made when a person died, so that the things the person owned could then be divided up according to their will.

JP (*see* Justice of the Peace)

Justice of the Peace a gentleman appointed to make sure that the law was carried out in the area he lived in

labourer a person who works for someone else doing work that does not need special training, like digging or carrying things

lepers people suffering from a bad skin disease called leprosy

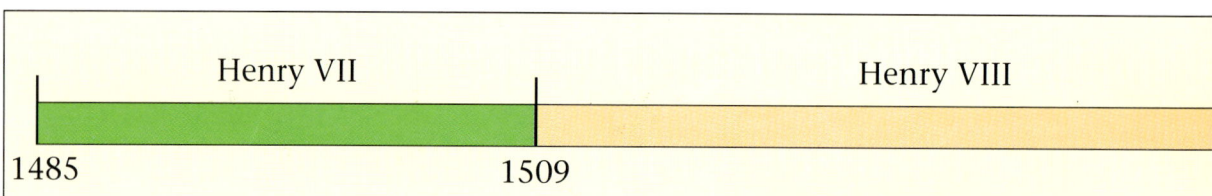

Henry VII	Henry VIII
1485	1509

licence a piece of paper giving a person permission to do something

master A person who an apprentice or other person works for. They have to obey their master, he has to look after them.

monarch a king or queen

noble belonging to an important family

official connected with people who are in charge of running things

overseer A person chosen to run something. Overseers of the poor ran the care for the poor, from collecting money to finding the poor work.

parish a part of a town or the country around a church, where everyone went to that church

passport a piece of paper given to a vagrant which said which part of the country they were caught in, and which part of the country they were born in, and so had to go back to

pillory A way of punishing people. They stood in public with their head and hands through holes in a wooden plank.

rate what a person was thought to be able to pay to help the poor, the richer people had to pay the biggest rate

rent To pay money to someone to use something. If a house is rented out, people live in it and pay the owner rent.

sewage water and toilet contents

slaughterhouse place where animals were killed for food

sturdy rogue someone able to work who was not working

stocks A way of punishing people. They sat in public with their feet through holes in a wooden plank.

trade buying and selling things, or a skilled job or profession

vagrant someone who has no home and no master and is wandering around the country

watchman person who walked round the streets at night, partly to make sure that nothing bad was going on, partly to call out the time

will a list that people make of what they want to happen to all their property (money, land and possessions) after they are dead

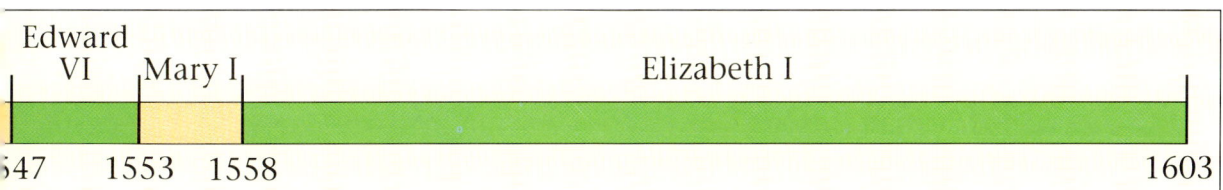

Edward VI	Mary I	Elizabeth I
547	1553 1558	1603

INDEX

Plain numbers (3) refer to the text. Bold numbers (**3**) refer to a source. Italic numbers (*3*) refer to a picture. Underlined numbers (3) refer to an information box.